मिस वर्ड

मिस योगिता

Made with ♥ on the Notion Press Platform
www.notionpress.com

क्रम-सूची

खण्ड 1

खण्ड 2

खण्ड 3

खण्ड 4

1. बहन ... 9

2. My Sister's Personality ... 12

3. My Lifeline ... 13

4. Indeed An Angel ... 14

5. My Sister ... 16

miss Yogita

The world's best sister

As many sisters, we weren't always best friends. I remember quarrels, screaming, door-slamming, but I couldn't have picked a better sister and a friend. Now that we are older, I can finally admit how happy I am to have grown up with such a great sister. Having a sister is one of the greatest things in life.

1
बहन

बहन का प्यार किसी दुआ से कम नहीं होता,
वो चाहे दूर भी हो तो कोई गम नहीं होता,
अक्सर रिश्ते दूरियों से फीके पड़ जाते है,
पर भाई बहन का प्यार कभी कम नहीं होता

मांगी थी दुआ हमने रब से..
देना मुझे एक प्यारी बहन जो अलग हो सबसे..
उस खुदा ने दे दी एक प्यारी सी बहन..
और कहाँ संभालो अनमोल है सबसे

फूलो का तारों का सबका कहना है..
एक हज़ार Kilo की मेरी बहना है

बहुत Lucky होते है वोह जिनको..
बहुत Care करने वाली Behan मिलती है

Yes! I'm नखरे वाली, क्यूंकि मेरे पास..
नखरे उठाने वाले Bhai जो हैं

#बहन से अच्छा #दोस्त और कोई नहीं हो सकता,
और मेरी #बहना तुमसे अच्छी कोई और #बहन हो ही नहीं सकती..

❧

सब से अलग हैं भैया मेरा, सब से प्यारा है भैया मेरा, कौन कहता हैं खुशियाँ ही सब होती हैं जहाँ में, मेरे लिए तो खुशियों से भी अनमोल हैं भैया मेरा....

❧

भाई अपनी बहन को तंग भी सब से ज्यादा करते है,
और अपनी बहनों से प्यार भी बहुत करते है

❧

बहन भाई की यारी सब से प्यारी और सब पे भारी

❧

#बेहन का #प्यार किसी #दुआ से कम नही होता,
#वो चाहे #दूर भी हो तो कोई #ग़म नही होता,
#अक्सर रिश्ते दुरियो से फीके पड़ जाते है,
#पर भाई #बहन का #प्यार कभी कम नहीं होता.

❧

#बहन वो #दोस्त है जो थामती तो #हाथ है,
पर स्पर्श #दिल को करती है..

❧

एक मैं Cute... एक मेरा भाई Cute...बाकी पूरी दुनिया डरावनी भूत
चाहें कितनी भी पतली क्यों न हो जाऊ...भाई हमेशा कहता हैं "कम खाया कर मोटी

❧

"कभी हमसे लड़ती है, कभी हमसे झगड़ती है, लेकिन बिना कहे हमारी हर बात को समझने का हुनर भी बहन ही रखती है
जिसके सर पर भाई का हाथ होता हैं. हर परेशानी में उसके साथ होता हैं, लड़ना झगड़ना फिर प्यार से मनाना तभी तो इस रिश्ते में इतना प्यार होता है

❧

बड़ा भाई बाप जैसा होता हैं और छोटा भाई दोस्त जैसा होता हैं. बहन की नजर में भाई किसी हीरो से कम नही होते हैं. भाई का प्यार किसी आशीर्वाद से कम नही होता है

❧

आज दिन बहुत खास है,
बहन के लिए कुछ मेरे पास है,
उसके सुकून के खातिर ओ बहना..
तेरे भाई हमेशा तेरे आस पास है

❧

तेरी मेरी बनती नहीं पर तेरे बिना
मेरी चलती भी नहीं... Love u..मोटी

❧

#खुशनसिब है वो #भाई जिसके #सर पर #बहन का हाथ होता है,
चाहे कुछ भी #हालात हो,
ये #रिस्ते हमेशा #साथ होता है..

❧

#बहन से अच्छा दोस्त और कोई नहीं हो सकता, और मेरी #Moti
तुमसे अच्छी कोई और #sister हो ही नहीं सकती.

❧

#बहन चाहे कितनी भी #पतली क्यों न हो,
#भाई हमेशा कहता #Moti ही बोलेगा.

❧

हां मैं #रावण बनना चाहूंगा..
जो #बहन के लिये #भगवान से भी टकरा जाये

❧

एक बहन का होना जीवन भर के लिए एक सबसे अच्छी दोस्त होने जैसा है।
हर हर वक्त मेरी बहन मेरा साथ दे ,
सब नकार दें मेरी बातों को पर वो अपना हाथ दे।

❧

2

My Sister's Personality

My sister has a very unique personality which is not seen commonly in today's world. She never judges anyone for their deeds. She is a religious person who believes we humans must not judge someone else as God will take care of it.

She has a bubbly personality and can brighten up the room wherever she goes. My sister is a sweet person who always tries to help out others. I have seen her help her friends all the time, even if they are acquaintances, she helps them equally.

Moreover, she is very lively. You will always find her playing around or goofing around with someone. She does not like sitting in one place, thus she is always all over the place. Further, she is very creative.

She has a solution to almost anything and everything. My sister has the special talent to find easy ways to do a difficult job. All of us always ask for her advice to simplify any kind of work.

I respect my sister for standing out of the crowd and always doing her own thing. Even if no one is doing it, she does not back off from doing the unique thing. She is my support system and inspiration.

Conclusion of My Sister Essay

All in all, I adore my sister a lot. She inspires me to become a better person and not judge anyone. As she is always empathetic towards animals, I also try my best to feed them and take care of them whenever possible. I hope to be a good sister to her and bring all the joy in her life.

3
My lifeline

My lifeline, in fact my world, indeed my everything
I just want to mention, that my sister is my world, my lifeline and everything to me, I want to tell you my sister that, when you are around world seems alright, everything seem just perfect. We as family are totally incomplete without you. One thing I could give you in my life, is the ability to see you through my eyes.

My sister is my idol without whom I simply cannot walk through my life. To explain the bonding it is as simple as that I am incomplete without my sister like a candle without light, a bus without tires, a mother without her child.

Please be always by my side. My sister is my mirror to life, who has always tried showing me the true paths of life. In the end all I want say is I love you the most. And will always work towards fulfilling the aim and dream of life living together always.

4
Indeed an angel

My sister is a sister, from different mother, being a sibling of her is in itself a great pleasure and a blessing from the god. A sister disguised in a sister-in-law is a cherry on the cake. Life have always given me some prodigious relationships in life, but my sister has always been a super power, my sense of strength, my angel for life.

My sister have always played different starring roles in my life, be it a mother, elder sibling, the younger sibling, cousin or as sister in law and hence I call my sister an angel, because I believe only an angel can play these many roles in one's life. A sister is somebody with whom you can share anything, anytime, anywhere without any hesitation.

The ever young beauty with brains is always admirable and a young scientist is always inspiring. My sister have always been a guiding book without whom, taking a step ahead is risky. I have always seen different advertisement where they show multiple hands of a women, the similar advertisement comes to my mind when i see my sister managing different things at a time. Hence my sister is an angel indeed.

Phases

My sister have always supported me all through my life, starting from my childhood, she has always been a hero to me.

My sister have been playing different roles in my life. And it is only she who can play these roles so perfectly at every point of life. My sister always have been brightening my life like a star. It is only her, with whom a real life "Hum aapke hain kaun" part 2 could be possible. It is only my sister who could be a sister, a friend, a mother, a sister-in-law, a teacher, actually a lifeline from the god.

The friend phase

My sister have always been my best friend ever, she can be called my 3' am friend. Yes, of course she have always been my friend without whom I cannot move a step ahead. Without a friend like her, life would have been the most monotonous.

She is the one without whom, a shopping is incomplete, visiting market is incomplete, going out for breakfast; lunch; dinner is incomplete, watching a movie is incomplete and what not. I feel totally incomplete without her.

5
My sister

Your brother
will never say he
loves you but
he loves you more
than anyone